Frank Lloyd Wright ®

DECORATIVE DESIGNS
A BOOK OF POSTCARDS

D0924537

Pomegranate

SAN FRANCISCO

Pomegranate Communications, Inc.
Box 6099, Rohnert Park, CA 94927
800-227-1428
www.pomegranate.com

Pomegranate Europe Ltd.
Fullbridge House, Fullbridge
Maldon, Essex CM9 4LE
England

ISBN 0-7649-1383-2
Pomegranate Catalog No. AA101

© The Frank Lloyd Wright Foundation, Taliesin West,
Scottsdale, Arizona. All rights reserved.

Pomegranate publishes books of
postcards on a wide range of subjects.
Please contact the publisher for more information.

Cover designed by Lisa Reid
Printed in China
09 08 07 06 05 04 03 02 01 00   10 9 8 7 6 5 4 3 2 1

To facilitate detachment of the postcards from this book, fold each card along its perforation line before tearing.

idely credited with revolutionizing American architecture, Frank Lloyd Wright (1867–1959) transformed steel, cement, wood, and glass into diaphanous, ethereal forms. Like a composer of music, he directed every element that went into his buildings, inside as well as outside. Furnishings and decorative arts were not afterthoughts but intrinsic parts of the architectural whole.

Wright loved to draw, and his graphic work combines a draftsman's technical mastery with the fluidity of a painter. Throughout his long career, he created hundreds of designs of astonishing imagination and beauty. At the age of sixty-one he wrote: "To this day I love to hold a handful of many colored pencils and open my hand to see them lying upon my palm, in the light." The thirty drawings in this book of postcards reveal the genius of this legendary master of architecture.

■ DECORATIVE DESIGNS

Ornamental Features

Tile mosaic pattern, 1902

Presentation drawing (detail). Ink and watercolor on board, 6¼ x 8⅛ in.

0205.001

Pomegranate

BOX 6099   ROHNERT PARK   CA 94927

© THE FRANK LLOYD WRIGHT FOUNDATION,
TALIESIN WEST, SCOTTSDALE, ARIZONA. ALL RIGHTS RESERVED

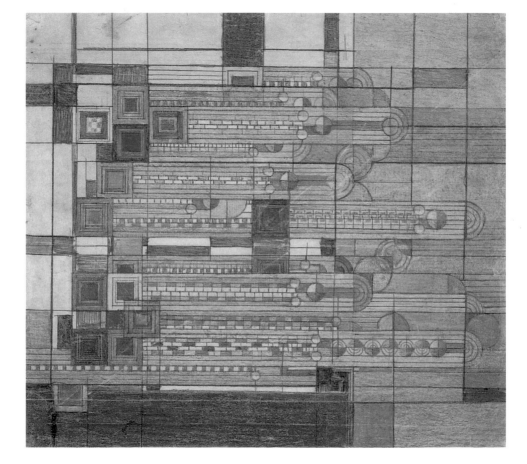

■ DECORATIVE DESIGNS

Saguaro Forms and Cactus Flowers

Cover design for *Liberty* magazine, 1926–27
Presentation drawing. Pencil and color pencil on tracing paper,
13 x 11¼ in.

2604.010

Pomegranate   BOX 6099   ROHNERT PARK   CA 94927

FRANK LLOYD WRIGHT® COLLECTION

© THE FRANK LLOYD WRIGHT FOUNDATION,
TALIESIN WEST, SCOTTSDALE, ARIZONA. ALL RIGHTS RESERVED

■ DECORATIVE DESIGNS

March Balloons
Rug design, 1955
Adapted from cover design for *Liberty* magazine, 1926–27
Presentation drawing. Pencil and color pencil on tracing paper, 28 x 24 in.
2604.003

CA 94927

ROHNERT PARK

BOX 6099

Pomegranate

© THE FRANK LLOYD WRIGHT FOUNDATION,
TALIESIN WEST, SCOTTSDALE, ARIZONA. ALL RIGHTS RESERVED

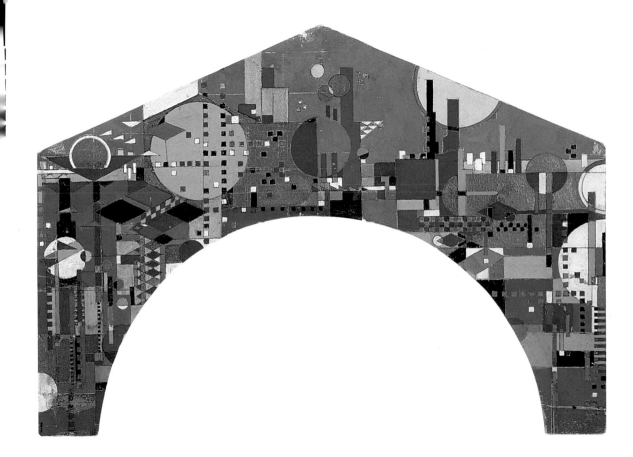

■ DECORATIVE DESIGNS

City by the Sea
Mural design for music pavilion, Taliesin West,
Scottsdale, Arizona, 1956
Tempera and gold paint on board, 21 x 27 in.
5609.001

BOX 6099   ROHNERT PARK   CA 94927

Pomegranate

© THE FRANK LLOYD WRIGHT FOUNDATION,
TALIESIN WEST, SCOTTSDALE, ARIZONA. ALL RIGHTS RESERVED

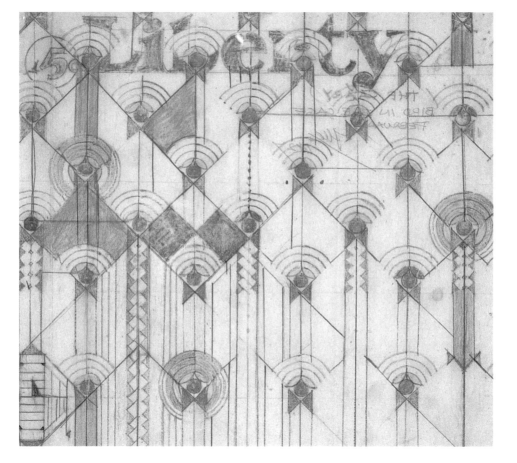

■ DECORATIVE DESIGNS

Bird in the Cage (Scherzo)
Cover design for *Liberty* magazine, 1926–27
Presentation drawing (detail). Pencil and color pencil on tracing
paper, 13 x 11¼ in.
2604.009

BOX 6099 ROHNERT PARK CA 94927

Pomegranate

© THE FRANK LLOYD WRIGHT FOUNDATION,
TALIESIN WEST, SCOTTSDALE, ARIZONA. ALL RIGHTS RESERVED

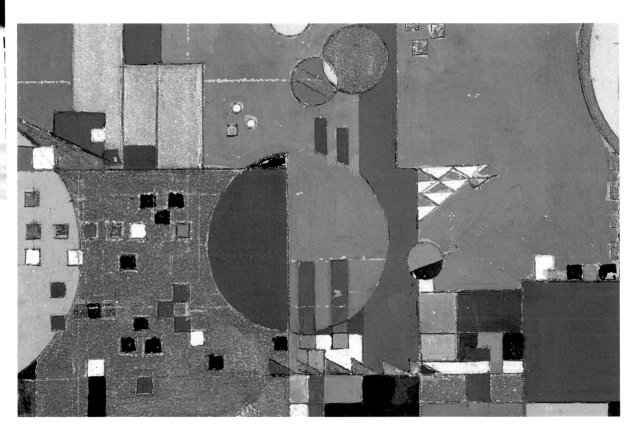

■ DECORATIVE DESIGNS

City by the Sea

Mural design (detail) for music pavilion, Taliesin West,
Scottsdale, Arizona, 1956
Tempera and gold paint on board, 21 x 27 in.
5609.001

BOX 6099   ROHNERT PARK   CA 94927

Pomegranate

© THE FRANK LLOYD WRIGHT FOUNDATION,
TALIESIN WEST, SCOTTSDALE, ARIZONA. ALL RIGHTS RESERVED

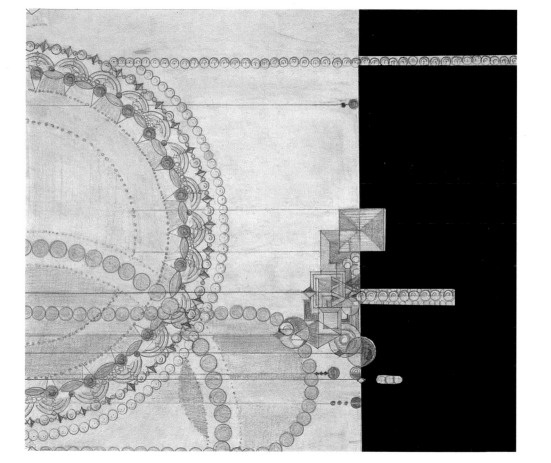

■ DECORATIVE DESIGNS

Jewelry Shop Window
Cover design for *Liberty* magazine, 1926–27
Presentation drawing. Pencil and color pencil on tracing paper,
12 x 12 in.
2709.001

Pomegranate

BOX 6099   ROHNERT PARK   CA 94927

FRANK
LLOYD
WRIGHT®
COLLECTION

© THE FRANK LLOYD WRIGHT FOUNDATION,
TALIESIN WEST, SCOTTSDALE, ARIZONA. ALL RIGHTS RESERVED

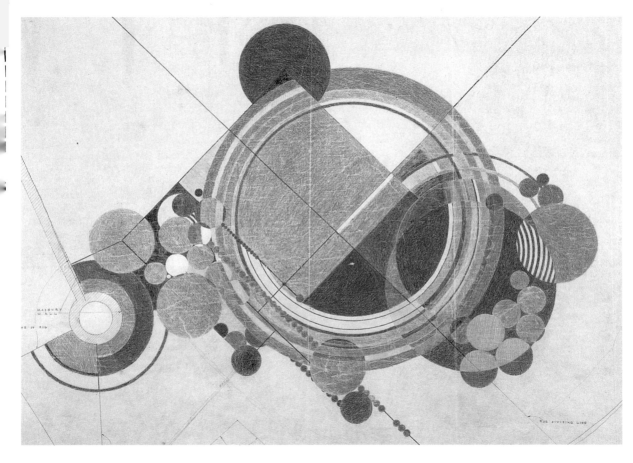

■ DECORATIVE DESIGNS

Rug design for David Wright house

Phoenix, Arizona, 1951

Presentation drawing (detail). Ink, pencil, and color pencil on tracing paper, 34 x 50¾ in.

5121.003

BOX 6099   ROHNERT PARK   CA 94927

Pomegranate

FRANK LLOYD WRIGHT® COLLECTION

© THE FRANK LLOYD WRIGHT FOUNDATION, TALIESIN WEST, SCOTTSDALE, ARIZONA. ALL RIGHTS RESERVED

SCALE ⅛" = 1'0"

HILLSIDE   ENTRANCE   GATE

FRANK   LLOYD   WRIGHT   ARCHITECT

■ Decorative Designs

Taliesin front gates

Hillside triangle, Taliesin, Spring Green, Wisconsin, 1939
Presentation drawing. Pencil and color pencil on tracing paper,
24½ x 31 in.

3921.002

BOX 6099   ROHNERT PARK   CA 94927

Pomegranate

© THE FRANK LLOYD WRIGHT FOUNDATION,
TALIESIN WEST, SCOTTSDALE, ARIZONA. ALL RIGHTS RESERVED

■ DECORATIVE DESIGNS

Rug design for Max Hoffman house
Rye, New York, 1957
Presentation drawing. Pencil and color pencil on tracing paper,
34 x 36 in.
5707.002

BOX 6099   ROHNERT PARK   CA 94927

Pomegranate

FRANK
LLOYD
WRIGHT®
COLLECTION

© THE FRANK LLOYD WRIGHT FOUNDATION,
TALIESIN WEST, SCOTTSDALE, ARIZONA. ALL RIGHTS RESERVED

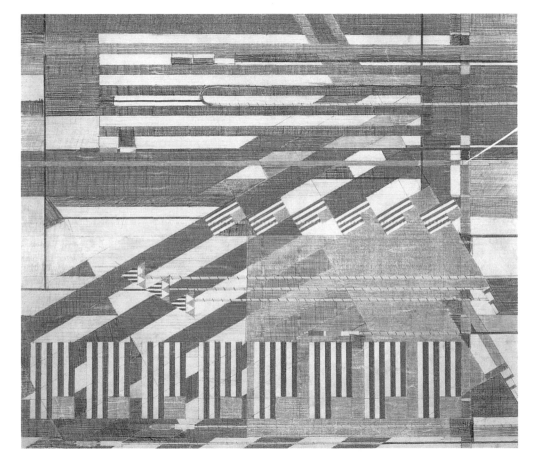

■ DECORATIVE DESIGNS

July Fourth
Rug design, 1955
Adapted from cover design for *Liberty* magazine, 1926–27
Presentation drawing. Pencil and color pencil on tracing paper,
28 x 24 in.
2604.004

BOX 6099   ROHNERT PARK   CA 94927

Pomegranate

FRANK
LLOYD
WRIGHT®
COLLECTION

© THE FRANK LLOYD WRIGHT FOUNDATION,
TALIESIN WEST, SCOTTSDALE, ARIZONA. ALL RIGHTS RESERVED

■ DECORATIVE DESIGNS

Rug design for Max Hoffman house
Rye, New York, 1957
Presentation drawing (detail). Pencil and color pencil on tracing
paper, 34 x 36 in.
5707.002

BOX 6099   ROHNERT PARK   CA 94927

Pomegranate

© THE FRANK LLOYD WRIGHT FOUNDATION,
TALIESIN WEST, SCOTTSDALE, ARIZONA. ALL RIGHTS RESERVED

FRANK LLOYD WRIGHT® COLLECTION

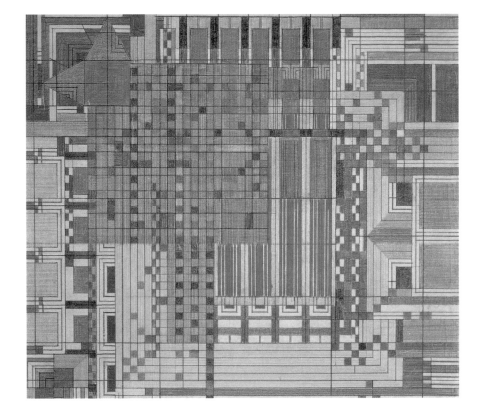

■ DECORATIVE DESIGNS

Old-Fashioned Window (Fugue)

Rug design, 1955
Adapted from cover design for *Liberty* magazine, 1926–27
Presentation drawing. Pencil and color pencil on tracing paper,
28 x 24 in.
2604.001

BOX 6099   ROHNERT PARK   CA 94927

Pomegranate

© THE FRANK LLOYD WRIGHT FOUNDATION,
TALIESIN WEST, SCOTTSDALE, ARIZONA. ALL RIGHTS RESERVED

FRANK
LLOYD
WRIGHT®
COLLECTION

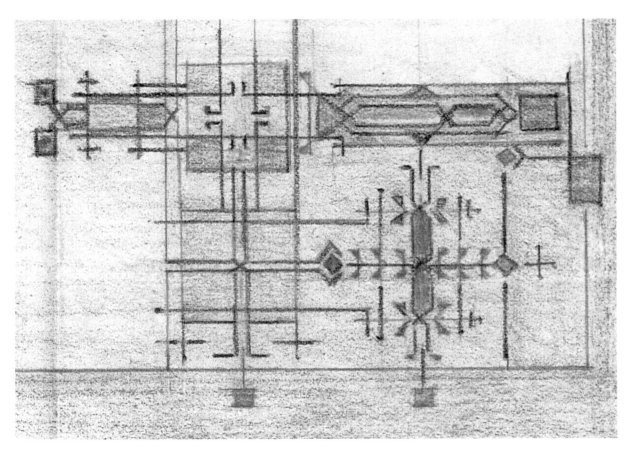

■ DECORATIVE DESIGNS

Early rug design
Rug corner pattern (detail), 1906
Pencil and color pencil on tracing paper, 11 × 12 in.
0620.005

BOX 6099   ROHNERT PARK   CA 94927

Pomegranate

© THE FRANK LLOYD WRIGHT FOUNDATION,
TALIESIN WEST, SCOTTSDALE, ARIZONA. ALL RIGHTS RESERVED

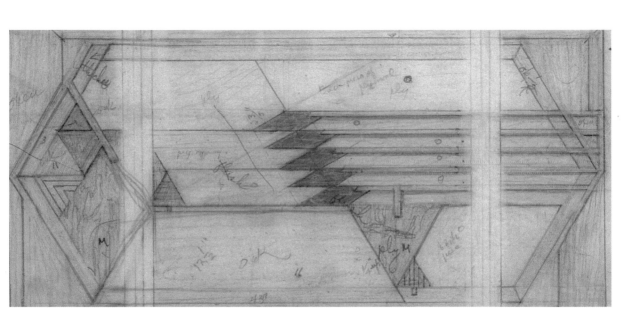

■ DECORATIVE DESIGNS

Fire screen in various scrap woods
Elevation (detail), Hillside, Taliesin, Spring Green, Wisconsin, 1934
Color pencil on tracing paper, 18 x 30 in.
3404.004

BOX 6099   ROHNERT PARK   CA 94927

Pomegranate

FRANK LLOYD WRIGHT® COLLECTION

© THE FRANK LLOYD WRIGHT FOUNDATION,
TALIESIN WEST, SCOTTSDALE, ARIZONA. ALL RIGHTS RESERVED

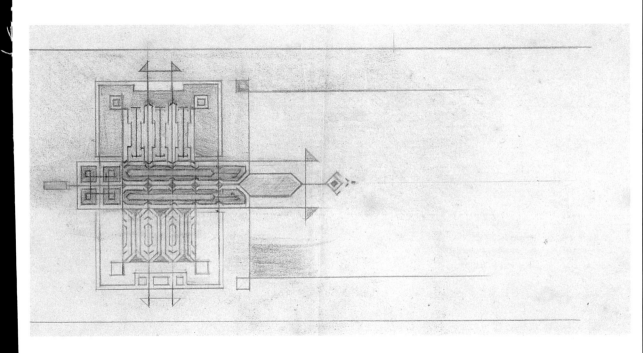

■ DECORATIVE DESIGNS

Early rug design
Rug pattern (detail), 1906
Color pencil on tracing paper, 14 x 12 in.
0620.006

Pomegranate

BOX 6099   ROHNERT PARK   CA 94927

© THE FRANK LLOYD WRIGHT FOUNDATION,
TALIESIN WEST, SCOTTSDALE, ARIZONA. ALL RIGHTS RESERVED

FRANK LLOYD WRIGHT® COLLECTION

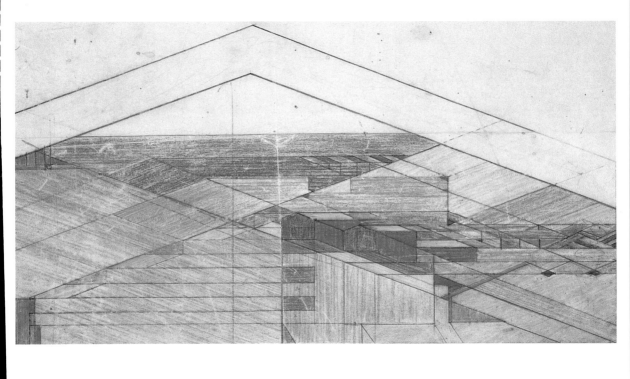

■ DECORATIVE DESIGNS

Wisconsin Red Barns

Mural for Hillside, Taliesin, Spring Green, Wisconsin, 1934
Elevation (detail). Color pencil on tracing paper, 17 x 18 in.

3404.003

BOX 6099   ROHNERT PARK   CA 94927

Pomegranate

© THE FRANK LLOYD WRIGHT FOUNDATION,
TALIESIN WEST, SCOTTSDALE, ARIZONA. ALL RIGHTS RESERVED

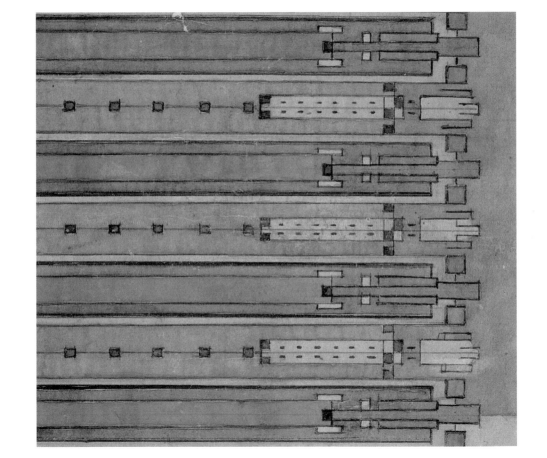

■ DECORATIVE DESIGNS

Rug design for Avery Coonley house
Riverside, Illinois, 1906–08
Presentation drawing. Watercolor, pencil, and ink on paper,
5⅞ x 7⅛ in.
0803.001

BOX 6099   ROHNERT PARK   CA 94927

Pomegranate

© THE FRANK LLOYD WRIGHT FOUNDATION,
TALIESIN WEST, SCOTTSDALE, ARIZONA. ALL RIGHTS RESERVED

FRANK
LLOYD
WRIGHT®
COLLECTION

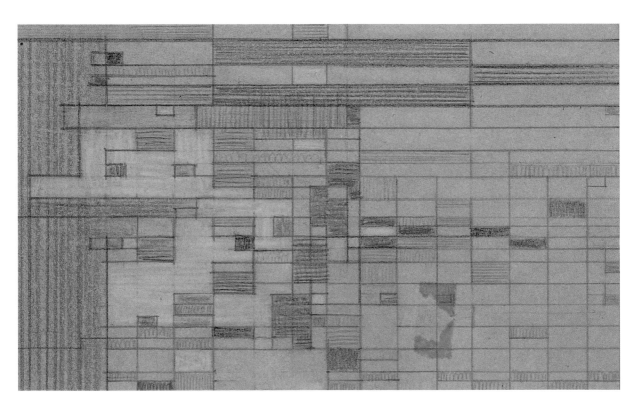

■ DECORATIVE DESIGNS

Early rug design
Rug pattern (detail), 1906
Color pencil on tracing paper, 14 x 14 in.
0620.008

BOX 6099   ROHNERT PARK   CA 94927

Pomegranate

© THE FRANK LLOYD WRIGHT FOUNDATION,
TALIESIN WEST, SCOTTSDALE, ARIZONA. ALL RIGHTS RESERVED

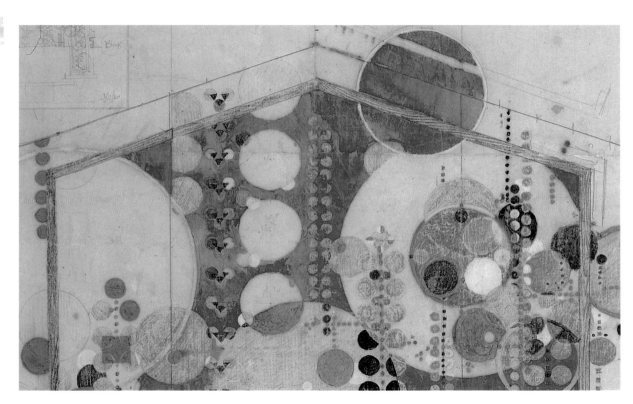

■ DECORATIVE DESIGNS

City by the Sea
Mural design (detail) for Midway Gardens, Chicago, Illinois, 1913–14
Pencil, color pencil, gold ink, watercolor, and crayon on tracing paper,
32½ × 30⅞ in.
1401.120

Pomegranate

BOX 6099   ROHNERT PARK   CA 94927

FRANK
LLOYD
WRIGHT®
COLLECTION

© THE FRANK LLOYD WRIGHT FOUNDATION,
TALIESIN WEST, SCOTTSDALE, ARIZONA. ALL RIGHTS RESERVED

◾ DECORATIVE DESIGNS

Carpet design

Rug pattern (detail) for Imperial Hotel, Tokyo, Japan, 1917
Pencil and color pencil on tracing paper, 45⅜ x 45⅜ in.
1509.044

BOX 6099   ROHNERT PARK   CA 94927

Pomegranate

© THE FRANK LLOYD WRIGHT FOUNDATION,
TALIESIN WEST, SCOTTSDALE, ARIZONA. ALL RIGHTS RESERVED

FRANK LLOYD WRIGHT®
COLLECTION

■ DECORATIVE DESIGNS

Machine-Age Ornament

Study for screen in plywood and copper, Hillside, Taliesin,
Spring Green, Wisconsin, 1934
Pencil and color pencil on tracing paper, 15 x 30 in.

3405.001

Pomegranate

BOX 6099   ROHNERT PARK   CA 94927

FRANK
LLOYD
WRIGHT®
COLLECTION

© THE FRANK LLOYD WRIGHT FOUNDATION,
TALIESIN WEST, SCOTTSDALE, ARIZONA. ALL RIGHTS RESERVED

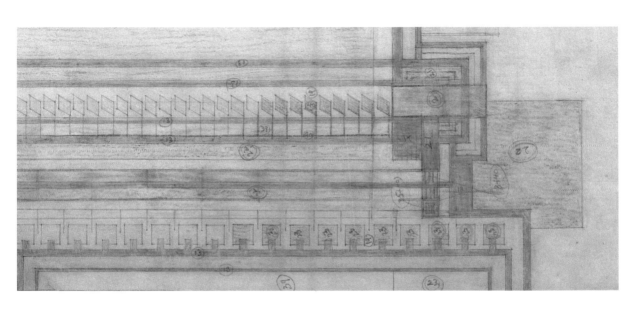

■ DECORATIVE DESIGNS

Carpet design
Rug pattern (detail) for Imperial Hotel, Tokyo, Japan, 1917
Pencil and color pencil on tracing paper, 29 x 17 in.
1509.068

BOX 6099   ROHNERT PARK   CA 94927

Pomegranate

FRANK LLOYD WRIGHT® COLLECTION

© THE FRANK LLOYD WRIGHT FOUNDATION,
TALIESIN WEST, SCOTTSDALE, ARIZONA. ALL RIGHTS RESERVED

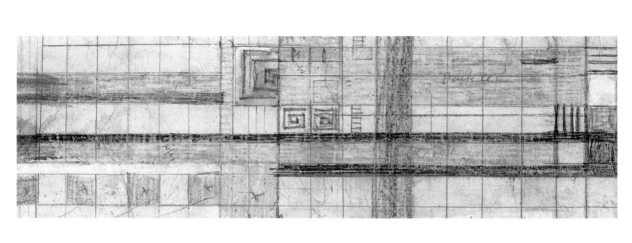

■ DECORATIVE DESIGNS

Theater Curtain I

Elevation (detail), Hillside Theater, Taliesin, Spring Green, Wisconsin, 1933
Pencil and color pencil on paper, 18⅝ x 26⅝ in.

3302.003

BOX 6099   ROHNERT PARK   CA 94927

Pomegranate

© THE FRANK LLOYD WRIGHT FOUNDATION,
TALIESIN WEST, SCOTTSDALE, ARIZONA. ALL RIGHTS RESERVED

FRANK LLOYD WRIGHT® COLLECTION

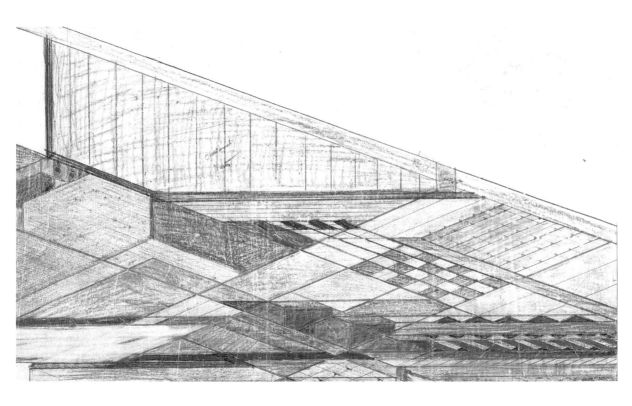

■ DECORATIVE DESIGNS

Wisconsin Red Barns
Mural design (detail) for Hillside, Taliesin, Spring Green, Wisconsin, 1934
Pencil and color pencil on tracing paper, 23 × 33 in.
3404.006

Pomegranate   BOX 6099   ROHNERT PARK   CA 94927

© THE FRANK LLOYD WRIGHT FOUNDATION,
TALIESIN WEST, SCOTTSDALE, ARIZONA. ALL RIGHTS RESERVED

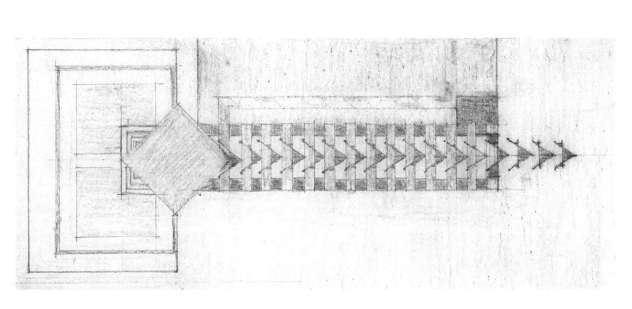

■ DECORATIVE DESIGNS

Carpet design for Promenade
Rug pattern (detail) for Imperial Hotel, Tokyo, Japan, 1917
Pencil and color pencil on tracing paper, 21 x 30 in.
1509.088

BOX 6099   ROHNERT PARK   CA 94927

Pomegranate

© THE FRANK LLOYD WRIGHT FOUNDATION,
TALIESIN WEST, SCOTTSDALE, ARIZONA. ALL RIGHTS RESERVED

■ DECORATIVE DESIGNS

Mural design
Untitled abstraction, Hillside, Taliesin, Spring Green, Wisconsin, 1934
Pencil and color pencil on tracing paper, 6 × 8 in.
3404.007

BOX 6099   ROHNERT PARK   CA 94927

Pomegranate

© THE FRANK LLOYD WRIGHT FOUNDATION,
TALIESIN WEST, SCOTTSDALE, ARIZONA. ALL RIGHTS RESERVED

FRANK
LLOYD
WRIGHT®
COLLECTION

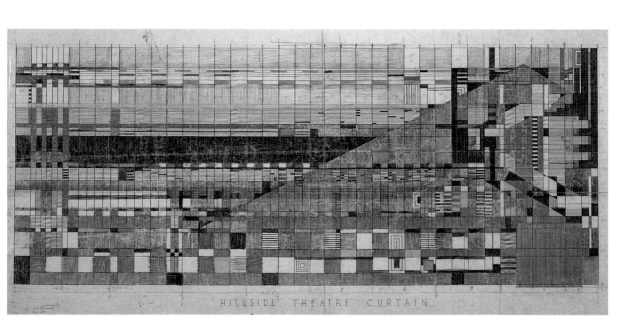

HILLSIDE THEATRE CURTAIN

■ DECORATIVE DESIGNS

Theater Curtain II (Wisconsin Landscape)

Elevation, Hillside Theater, Taliesin, Spring Green, Wisconsin, 1952
Pencil and color pencil on tracing paper, 36 x 58 in.

5223.002

BOX 6099   ROHNERT PARK   CA 94927

Pomegranate

FRANK
LLOYD
WRIGHT®
COLLECTION

© THE FRANK LLOYD WRIGHT FOUNDATION,
TALIESIN WEST, SCOTTSDALE, ARIZONA. ALL RIGHTS RESERVED

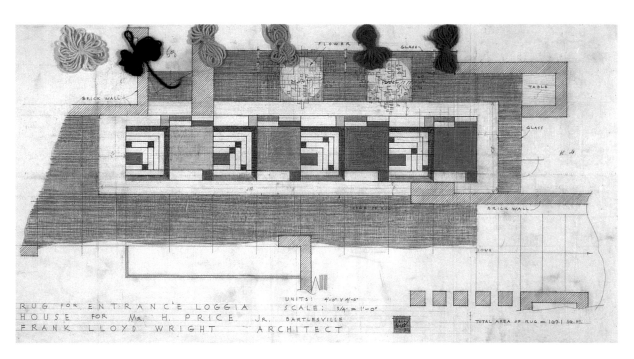

FLOWER   GLASS

BRICK WALL

TABLE

GLASS

BRICK WALL

DOWN

UNITS: 4'-0" X 4'-0"
RUG FOR ENTRANCE LOGGIA   SCALE: 3/4" = 1'-0"
HOUSE FOR MR. H. PRICE JR. BARTLESVILLE
FRANK LLOYD WRIGHT   ARCHITECT   TOTAL AREA OF RUG = 169.1 SQ. FT.

■ DECORATIVE DESIGNS

Rug design for Harold Price Jr. house

Bartlesville, Oklahoma, 1954–55
Presentation drawing. Pencil and color pencil on tracing paper, 7 x 35 in.
5420.005

BOX 6099   ROHNERT PARK   CA 94927

Pomegranate

FRANK
LLOYD
WRIGHT®
COLLECTION

© THE FRANK LLOYD WRIGHT FOUNDATION,
TALIESIN WEST, SCOTTSDALE, ARIZONA. ALL RIGHTS RESERVED

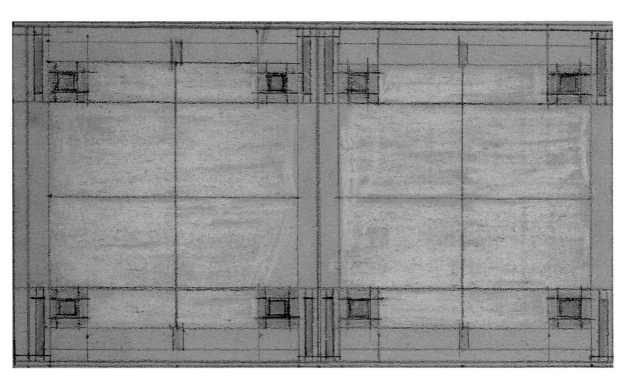

■ DECORATIVE DESIGNS

Art glass ceiling panel
Unity Temple, Oak Park, Illinois, 1905–08
Presentation drawing (detail). Pencil and crayon on paper,
6 x 12¼ in.
0611.107

Pomegranate

BOX 6099   ROHNERT PARK   CA 94927

© THE FRANK LLOYD WRIGHT FOUNDATION,
TALIESIN WEST, SCOTTSDALE, ARIZONA. ALL RIGHTS RESERVED

FRANK
LLOYD
WRIGHT®
COLLECTION

Pomegranate Books of Postcards
on Art, Architecture, and Design

Pomegranate publishes books of postcards on a wide range of subjects.
Please write to the publisher for more information.

FRANK LLOYD WRIGHT COLLECTION

- © 2 0 0 0 -
THE FRANK LLOYD WRIGHT
F O U N D A T I O N
- TALIESIN WEST -
- SCOTTSDALE, ARIZONA -
- ALL RIGHTS RESERVED -

$9.95 ($13.95 CAN.) AA101

ISBN 0-7649-1383-2

7 17194 00101 9

9 780764 913839

FRANK LLOYD WRIGHT: DECORATIVE DESIGNS

Seeking perfection in every ornament, Frank Lloyd Wright designed exquisite patterns for the rugs, carpets, murals, and mosaics that adorned his architectural masterpieces. These dazzling, highly abstract works of graphic art reflect Wright's lifelong fascination with geometric motifs, which he believed represented specific principles: the circle symbolized infinity; the triangle, structural unity; the spire, aspiration; the spiral, organic progress; and the square, integrity. Wright sought to convey the unity of nature and spirit through these forms, developing a vocabulary of design renowned for its elegance and genius.

This postcard book features thirty of Wright's most ima textile, window, and mural designs; it also includes several created for the cover of *Liberty* magazine. ∎

CONTAINS THIRTY OVERSIZED POSTCA

T3-ADP-868